AMAZING AFRICA: A-Z

BY: DR. ARTIKA R. TYNER
& MONICA HABIA

All inquiries or sales requests should be addressed to:

Planting People Growing Justice Press
P.O. Box 131894
Saint Paul, MN 55113
www.ppgjli.org

Printed in China

First Edition
LCCN: 2018944900
HC ISBN: 978-0-9985553-3-1
SC ISBN: 978-0-9985553-2-4

This book is dedicated to the children of Africa.

—A.T. and M.H.

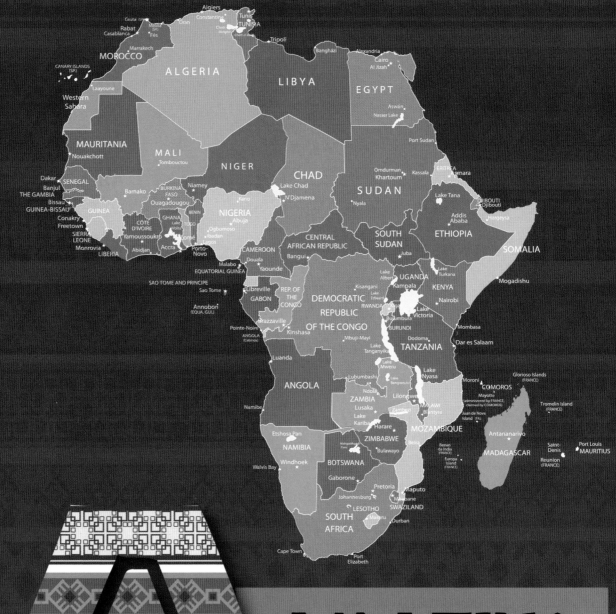

AMAZING AFRICA

There are **54** countries in the continent of Africa.

BEACHES

The sun glistening on the white sand of the beaches of Freetown, Sierra Leone.

CHILDREN OF AFRICA

Children play ampe, love to dance, and enjoy singing.

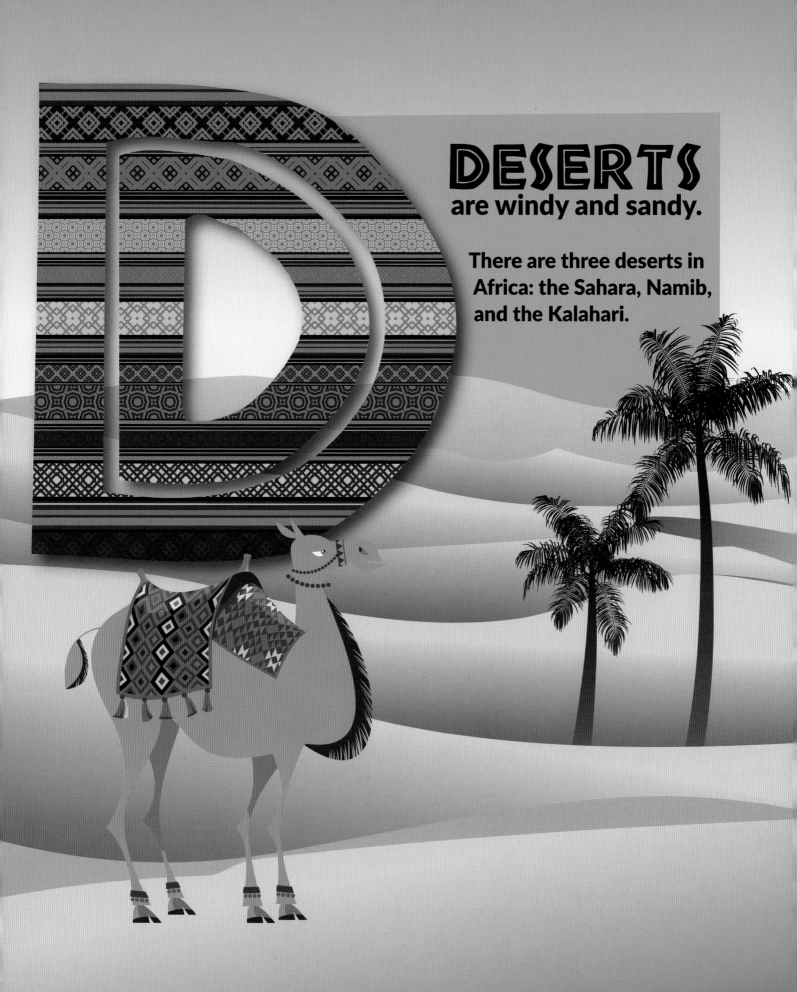

DESERTS
are windy and sandy.

There are three deserts in Africa: the Sahara, Namib, and the Kalahari.

"EDUCATION  is the most powerful weapon which you can use to change the world." – *Nelson Mandela*

In Africa, students study and train to become doctors, lawyers, engineers, entrepreneurs, writers, and world leaders.

FOOD

reflects the rich culture of Africa. Most foods are grain, vegetable, meat, and fish based. Fufu and Garri are popular in the West Africa regions and mostly eaten with soup or sauce. Ugali, Jollof rice, Akara, Sambosa, and Suya are all very tasteful African foods to try.

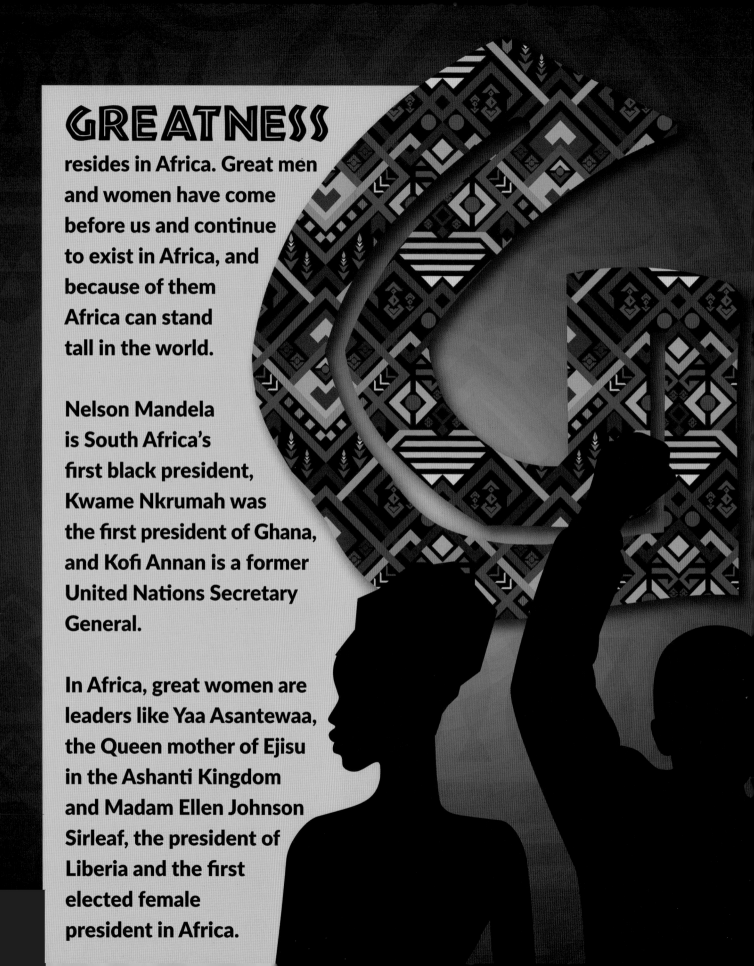

GREATNESS

resides in Africa. Great men and women have come before us and continue to exist in Africa, and because of them Africa can stand tall in the world.

Nelson Mandela is South Africa's first black president, Kwame Nkrumah was the first president of Ghana, and Kofi Annan is a former United Nations Secretary General.

In Africa, great women are leaders like Yaa Asantewaa, the Queen mother of Ejisu in the Ashanti Kingdom and Madam Ellen Johnson Sirleaf, the president of Liberia and the first elected female president in Africa.

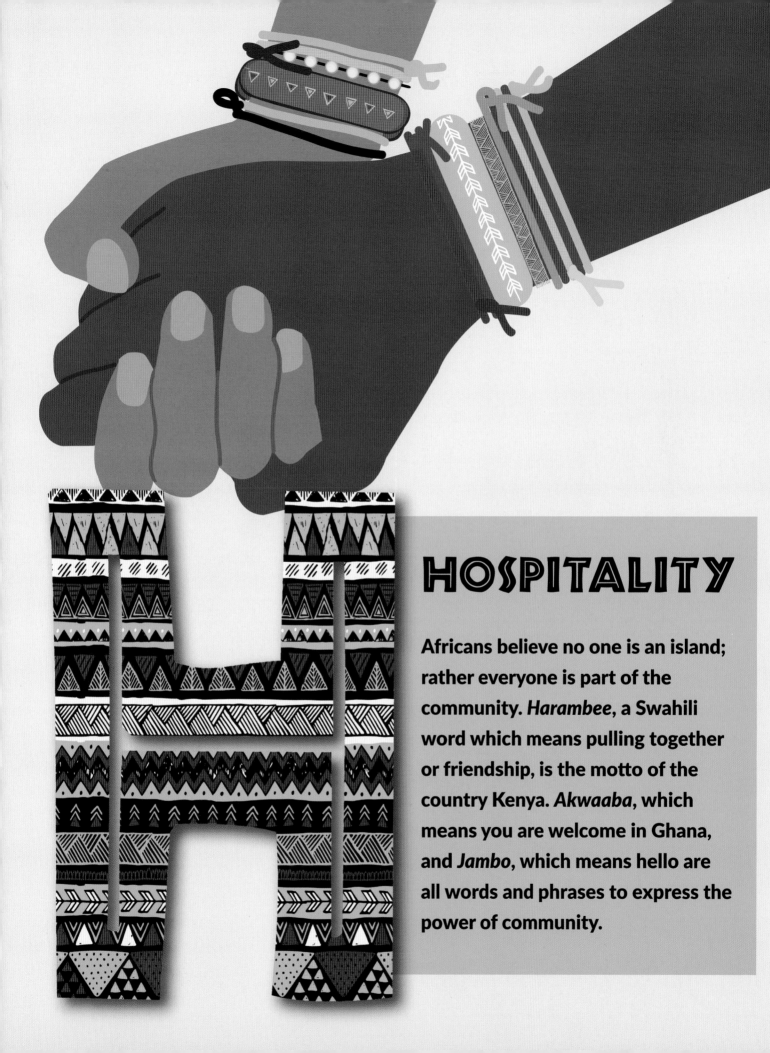

HOSPITALITY

Africans believe no one is an island; rather everyone is part of the community. *Harambee*, a Swahili word which means pulling together or friendship, is the motto of the country Kenya. *Akwaaba*, which means you are welcome in Ghana, and *Jambo*, which means hello are all words and phrases to express the power of community.

INDEPENDENCE

Many African countries were colonized by European countries. This means that African countries had to fight to be free and independent of these countries.

JOHANNESBURG

is a beautiful city in South Africa. Like many parts of the world, Africa has beautiful cities too. Some of them are: The Cape Town of South Africa, Nairobi of Kenya, Lagos of Nigeria, Accra of Ghana, Kigali of Rwanda, and Dar es Salaam of Tanzania.

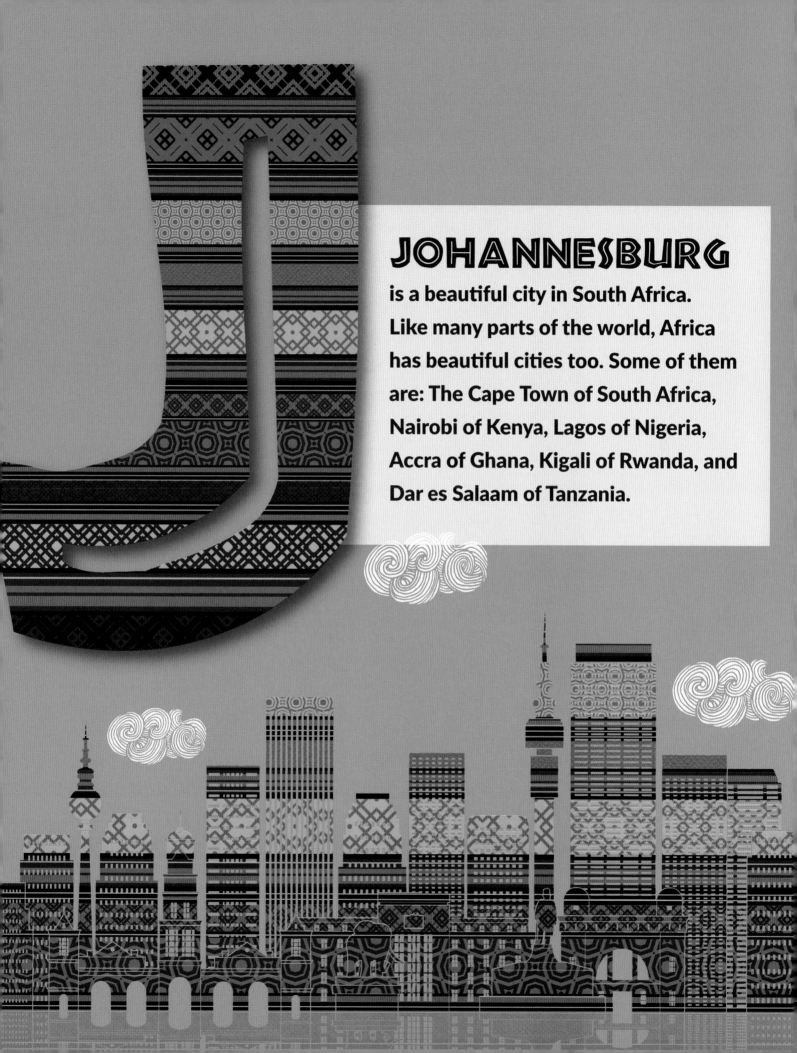

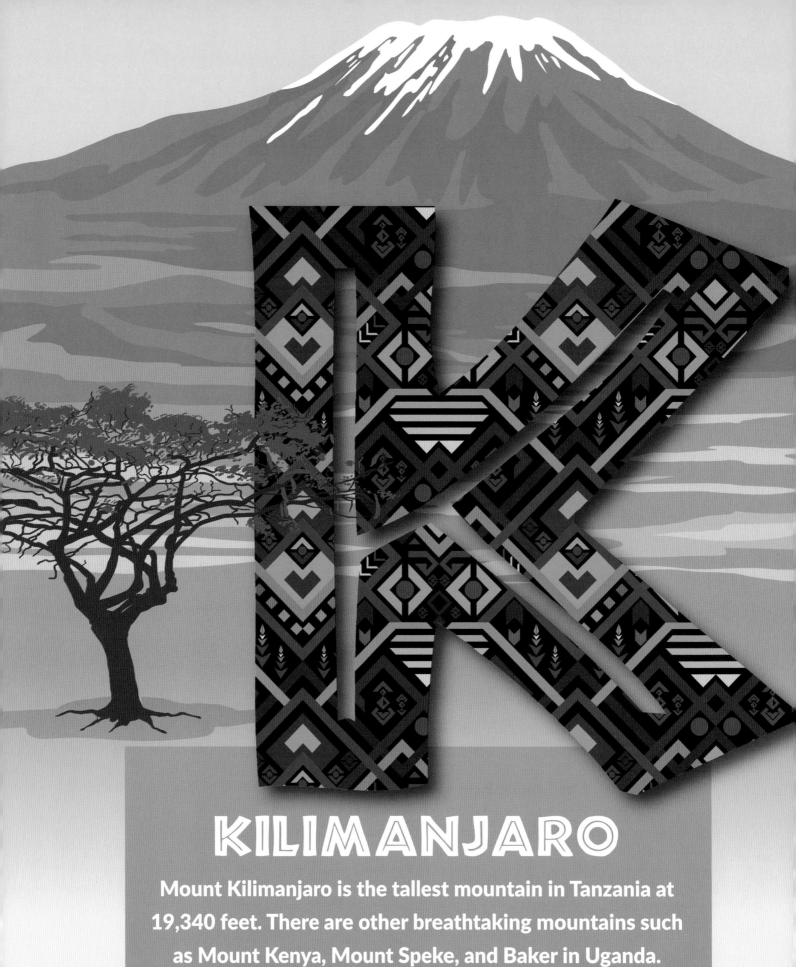

KILIMANJARO

Mount Kilimanjaro is the tallest mountain in Tanzania at 19,340 feet. There are other breathtaking mountains such as Mount Kenya, Mount Speke, and Baker in Uganda.

LANGUAGES

There are over 1,000 languages spoken throughout Africa. It is very common for Africans to speak two or more languages.

MAMA AFRICA

is her name. Her claim to fame is being the Earth's oldest populated area. Civilization began in Africa. Africa is the second largest continent in the world.

NATURE

is Africa and Africa is nature. Aside from the rivers and mountains, Africa boasts of unique mammals, birds, reptiles, fish, insects, and plants.

OUGUIYA

is Mauritania's currency. As the dollar equates to America, Naira is to Nigeria, and Cedi is to Ghana.

P

PROVERBS

are wise sayings and form

part of the African culture.

"Wisdom is like
a baobab tree,
no one individual
can embrace it."

– Ghanaian proverb

EGYPT

●
QUENĀ

QUENĀ
is a city in Egypt.

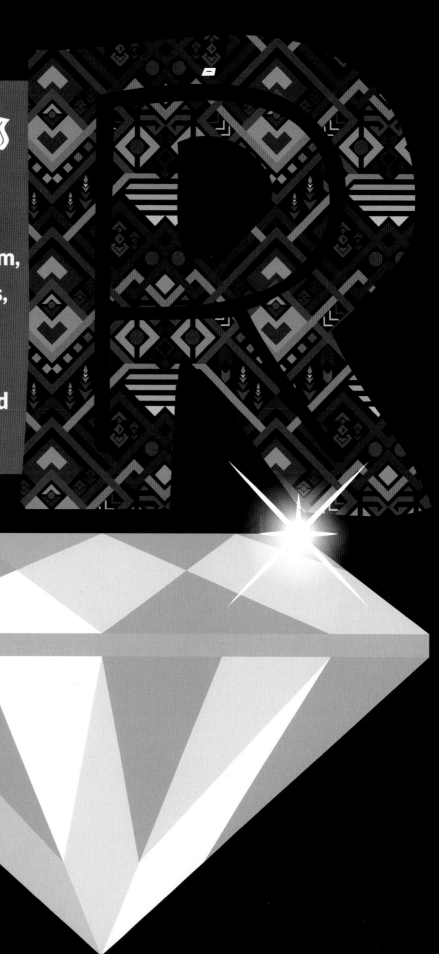

RESOURCES are in abundance in Africa, most of them natural. Gold, petroleum, diamonds, cocoa beans, silver, and bauxite are just a few of the many natural resources found on the continent.

SLAVERY

During the trans-Saharan and East African slave trades, strong and able men and women from Africa were sold into slavery.

TRIBES are largely spread across Africa and connect families, communities, and ethnic groups together.

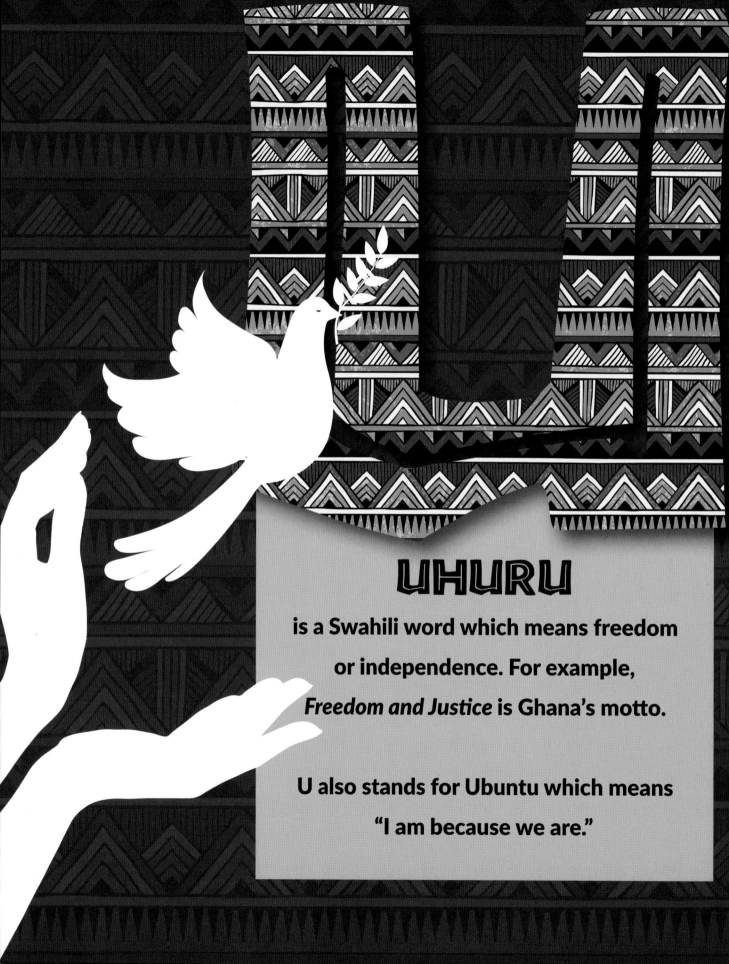

UHURU

is a Swahili word which means freedom
or independence. For example,
Freedom and Justice is Ghana's motto.

U also stands for Ubuntu which means
"I am because we are."

VICTORIA FALLS is the world's largest waterfall and it is located on the Zambezi River.

WRITERS

The world celebrates great writers and Africa can boast of many like Chinua Achebe of Nigeria and Ayi Kwei Armah of Ghana.

XHOSA is the second largest ethnic group in South Africa after the Zulus. It is also one of the official languages of South Africa.

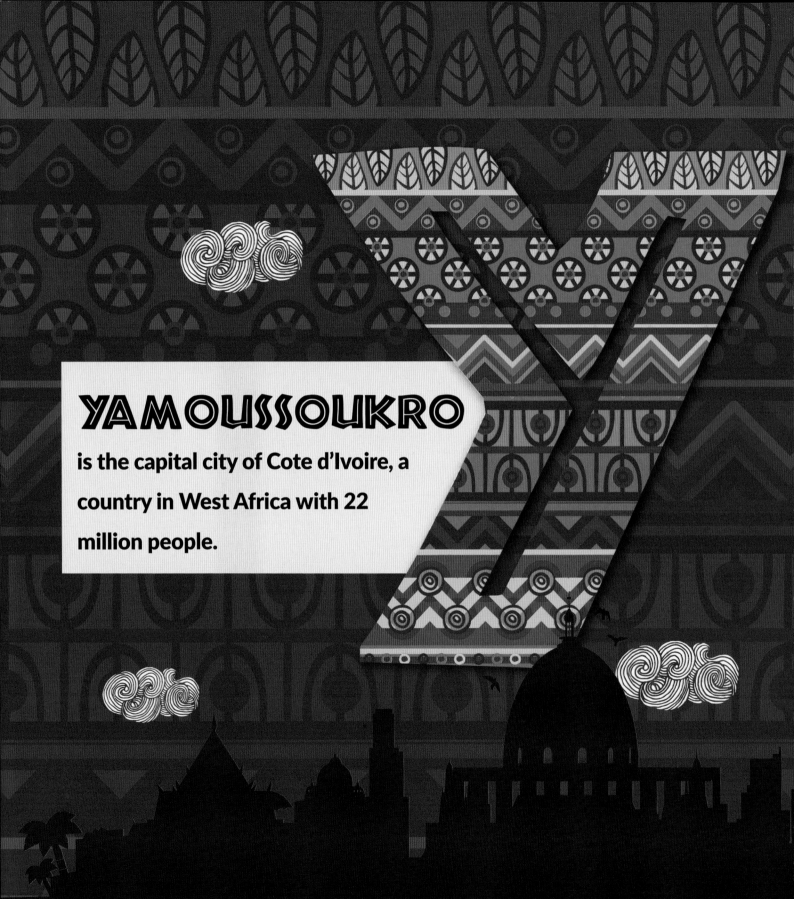

YAMOUSSOUKRO

is the capital city of Cote d'Ivoire, a country in West Africa with 22 million people.

ZAMBEZI RIVER is the fourth longest river in Africa. Lake Kariba is one of the biggest man-made lakes in the world.

MAP OF AFRICA

LIST OF COUNTRIES (A-Z)

A is for Algeria and Angola

B is for Benin, Botswana, Burkina Faso, and Burundi

C is for Cameroon, Cape Verde, Central African Republic, Chad, Comoros, Democratic Republic of the Congo, Republic of the Congo and Cote d'Ivoire

D is for Djibouti

E is for Egypt, Equatorial Guinea, Eritrea, and Ethiopia

G is Gabon, Gambia, Ghana, Guinea, and Guinea Bissau

K is for Kenya

L is for Lesotho, Liberia, and Libya

M is for Madagascar, Malawi, Mali, Mauritania, Mauritius, Morocco, and Mozambique

N is for Namibia, Niger, and Nigeria

R is for Rwanda

S is for Sao Tome and Principe, Senegal, Seychelles, Sierra Leone, Somalia, South Africa, South Sudan, Sudan, and Swaziland

T is Tanzania, Togo, and Tunisia

U is for Uganda

Z is for Zambia and Zimbabwe

OTHER AMAZING FACTS ABOUT AFRICA

Africa has the **second largest population in the world** with 1.216 billion people as of 2016. Nigeria is the most populated country with 181 million and Seychelles has 94,737 people.

River Nile is the **longest river in Africa** and the world. It flows through countries such as Uganda, Ethiopia, Sudan, and Egypt.

The Niger River is the **third longest river in Africa**. It flows through Mali, Niger, and Nigeria. It is referred to as the principal river of Western Africa.

Regions of Africa: The 54 countries are divided into 5 regions depending on their locations in East, West, North, South, and Central Africa.

Uganda is the **only country** in Africa which starts with the letter "U" and Swahili is one of the languages spoken by Ugandans.

AFRICAN PROVERBS

On Education:

"If you think education is expensive,
try ignorance."

– African proverb

On Listening:

"The fool speaks, the wise listens."

– Ethiopian proverb

On Community:

"If you want to go quickly, go alone,
if you want to go far, go together."

– African proverb

On Team-building:

"Unity is strength, division is weakness."

– Swahili proverb

Dr. Artika Tyner:

Dr. Artika Tyner (a.k.a. Miss Freedom Fighter, Esquire) is a passionate educator, award-winning author, civil rights attorney, sought after speaker, and advocate for justice who is committed to helping children discover their leadership potential and serve as change agents in the global community. She is the Founder/ CEO of Planting People Growing Justice Leadership Institute.

Monica Yaa Habia:

Monica Yaa Habia was born and raised in Ghana. She believes in the power of a quality education and is committed to bridge the knowledge gap of Africa through her writings and research. She currently lives in Minnesota and is a program design and support professional for organizations including non-profits.

About Planting People Growing Justice Leadership Institute

Planting People Growing Justice Leadership Institute seeks to plant seeds of social change through education, training, and community outreach.

A portion of proceeds from this book will support the educational programming of Planting People Growing Justice Leadership Institute.

Learn more at www.ppgjli.org

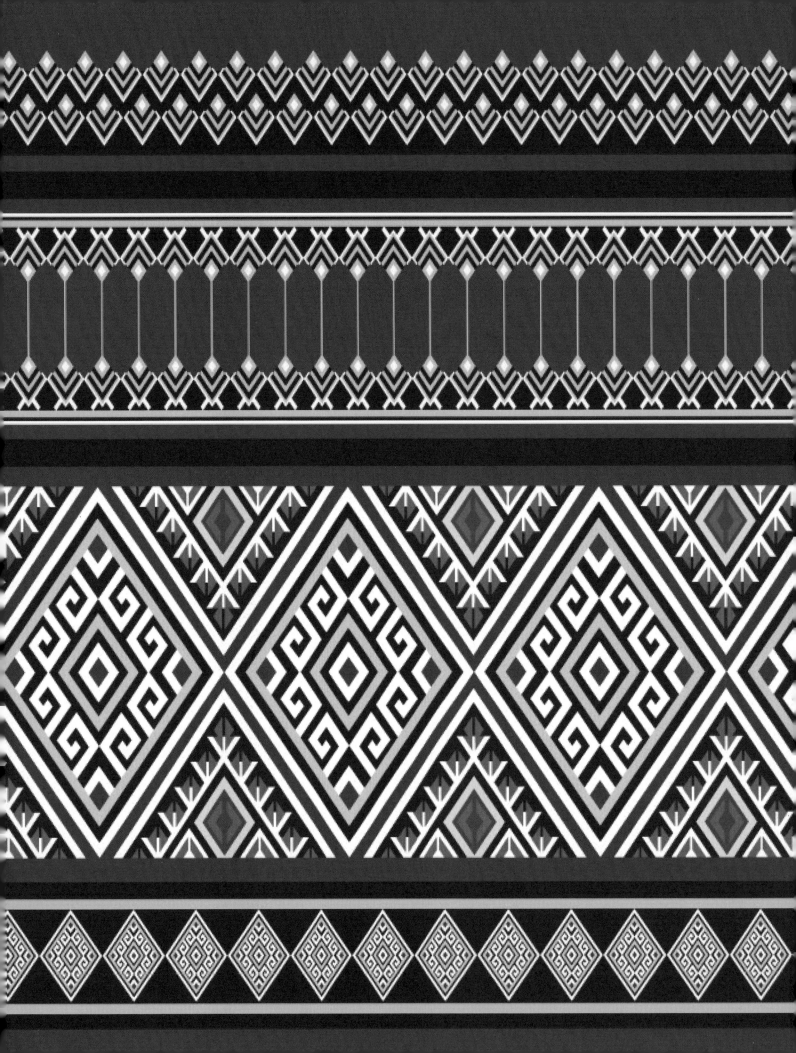